GREAT INVENTIONS

RADIO AND TELEVISION

By Michael Teitelbaum

WORLD ALMANAC® LIBRARY

Please visit our web site at: www.worldalmanaclibrary.com
For a free color catalog describing World Almanac® Library's list of high-quality books
and multimedia programs, call 1-800-848-2928 (USA) or 1-800-387-3178 (Canada).
World Almanac® Library's fax: (414) 332-3567.

Library of Congress Cataloging-in-Publication Data

Teitelbaum, Michael.
    Radio and television / by Michael Teitelbaum.
        p. cm. — (Great inventions)
    Includes bibliographical references and index.
    ISBN 0-8368-5802-6 (lib. bdg.)
    1. Radio—History—Juvenile literature.   2. Television—History—Juvenile
literature.   3. Broadcasting—History—Juvenile literature.   I. Title.
TK6550.7.T45   2005
384.54—dc22   2004056932

First published in 2005 by
World Almanac® Library
330 West Olive Street, Suite 100
Milwaukee, WI 53132 USA

Copyright © 2005 by World Almanac® Library.

A Creative Media Applications, Inc. Production
Design and Production: Alan Barnett, Inc.
Editors: Matt Levine, Susan Madoff
Copy Editor: Laurie Lieb
Proofreader: Laurie Lieb
Indexer: Nara Wood
World Almanac® Library editorial direction: Mark J. Sachner
World Almanac® Library editor: Gini Holland
World Almanac® Library art direction: Tammy West
World Almanac® Library production: Jessica Morris

Photo credits: © AP/Wide World Photos: pages 4, 7, 8, 16, 20, 22, 28, 32, 34, 38,
39, 41, 42; © Bettmann/CORBIS: pages 5, 6, 12, 13, 14, 18, 24, 31, 33, 37;
© Hulton-Deutsch Collection/ CORBIS: page 11; diagrams by Rolin Graphics: page 15.

Printed in Canada

1 2 3 4 5 6 7 8 9 09 08 07 06 05

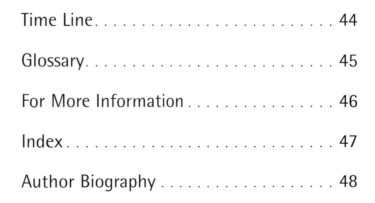

TABLE OF CONTENTS

Words that appear in the glossary are printed in **boldface** type the first time they appear in the text.

Today, people live in a world of instant entertainment. Turn on a satellite radio **receiver** and choose from hundreds of stations. Turn on the television and choose from hundreds of channels, movies on demand, or DVDs. In the early days of radio and television, however, there were few channels to choose from, and not everyone had the radio and TV sets needed to receive broadcast signals.

Before the invention of radio, messages had to be carried over wires. Telephones brought voices from one part of the world to another. Before telephones, telegraphs sent messages as a series of electronic beeps that stood for the letters of the alphabet. Before the telegraph, the only way to get a message from one place to another was to use signal flags or fires, which could be seen over long distances—or, of course, to physically carry the message on foot or horseback.

▲ The telecommunications industry is continually working on technology to improve the everyday items in our lives. In 2003, Sanyo introduced a new mobile phone that can receive digital TV signals.

Telegraph and Telephone

The invention of the telegraph by Samuel F. B. Morse (1791–1872) in 1844 radically changed the way the world communicated. Detailed messages could now be sent across vast distances almost **instantaneously**. Anywhere a telegraph wire could be strung, including under the ocean, this long-distance communication was possible. An electronic signal generated by a telegraph key traveled through the wire and emerged as a beeping sound in the headphones of a person on the other end of the wire. The number and length of beeps were coded so that they could be interpreted as letters of the alphabet.

In the 1870s, an inventor named Alexander Graham Bell (1847–1922) realized that music and human voices could be sent across telegraph wires, too. In 1876, Bell transmitted his own voice over a telegraph line, effectively inventing the telephone. Now, people on different continents could actually speak to each other. Bell's telephone also opened the possibility that if speech could be brought into people's homes, so could music and other types of entertainment.

The telegraph and telephone were still limited by the need for wires to carry the messages from one point to another. The next step in the evolution of worldwide communications would be to make a wireless system.

Building Blocks

In the early 1800s, scientists Michael Faraday (1791–1867), from England, and Joseph Henry (1797–1878), from the United States, each independently discovered that an electric current could jump from one wire to another wire even though the two wires weren't touching. This discovery was the first baby step toward the invention of radio.

In 1873, a Scottish physicist named James Clerk Maxwell (1831–1879) published his theory on how electric current traveled from wire to wire. Maxwell's

James Clerk Maxwell (1831–1879)

James Clerk Maxwell published his first scientific paper at the age of fifteen (on methods of drawing oval curves). He was a professor of philosophy, physics, and astronomy from 1847 to 1855. He also wrote mathematical formulas explaining Faraday's experiments with electromagnetism. Some of Maxwell's formulas on the movement of electromagnetic waves later helped Albert Einstein (1879–1955) develop his famous theory of relativity.

Michael Faraday (1791–1867)

Michael Faraday was born in London, England, in 1791. As a boy, he was apprenticed to a bookbinder and soon developed a love of science. He left his apprenticeship to work for a scientist named Humphry Davy. In the 1820s, Faraday began experimenting with electromagnetic waves, which would eventually form the basis of radio. He discovered that electrical energy could be used to move objects. This led to Faraday's invention of the electric motor. This photograph shows the inventor and his wife observing one of his experiments.

theory was that electric current in the first wire produced a force in the air called a **magnetic field**. Such fields moved through the air until they reached something that conducted electricity, such as the second wire. Maxwell called these ripples of magnetic fields **electromagnetic waves**. Although his theories impressed the scientific community, Maxwell never did any practical experiments to prove his claims.

In the late 1880s, a German physicist named Heinrich Hertz (1857–1894) set up an experiment that actually produced electromagnetic waves. Hertz sent these waves, visible as sparks, from one coil of wire (a **transmitter**) to another coil of wire (a receiver) across a room. In time, these waves would come to be known as radio waves.

Marconi's Inspiration

In 1890, a sixteen-year-old Italian named Guglielmo Marconi (1874–1937) read of Hertz's work. Marconi imagined how electromagnetic waves could be used to send messages great distances without the use of wires. Distance and the need for wires would no longer keep people from communicating with each other from anywhere. Marconi set to work on the invention that would change communication and entertainment around the world. His imagination and ambition would soon pay off.

The Hertz

In honor of Heinrich Hertz's experiments that confirmed the existence of electromagnetic waves, the unit used for measuring the frequency of these waves is known as the *hertz*. The hertz measures the frequency of a radio wave, which is the number of times the wave completes a cycle in one second.

Marconi hoped to take the existing communications technology—the telegraph—and eliminate the need for wires. Marconi went to work in a laboratory he built in the attic of his parents' home in Italy. He found he could boost the power of his signal by placing metal plates near his transmitter and receiver. These metal plates were soon replaced by long strands of copper wire, forming the first primitive radio antenna. Gradually, Marconi increased the power of both his transmission device and his receiver, moving outside as his equipment grew larger and more unwieldy. By 1896, Marconi was able to successfully send and receive wireless telegraph signals over a distance of 2 miles (3.2 kilometers).

Marconi's mother, who was Irish, took him to England, where he gained the backing of the British government and secured a **patent** for his wireless telegraph system. Within a year, he had formed the British Marconi Company. Marconi

▼ In this 1901 photograph, Guglielmo Marconi tests radio signals for ship-to-shore communication.

also kept improving his system. In 1899, he sent a signal across the English Channel, from England to France. That same year, he journeyed to the United States and sold his equipment to shipping companies. These companies used Marconi's system to remain in contact with ships at sea.

In 1901, Marconi sent the first transatlantic wireless signal 2,000 miles (3,220 km), from England to Newfoundland. The same year, Marconi returned to the United States to form the American Marconi Company. Marconi had started a revolution in communications. Ship-to-shore communication was now possible. Governments around the world began to use the technology for their military and police forces. Soon, businesses would use this new long-distance wireless system to communicate worldwide and gain an advantage over their competition.

Lee De Forest and the Audion Tube

One American who took great interest in the work of Marconi was Dr. Lee De Forest (1873–1961) from Council Bluffs, Iowa. After receiving his doctoral degree with a thesis written about radio waves, De Forest set up a laboratory and began working on ways to improve the power and reception of these waves.

Early radio transmitters and receivers were large and cumbersome, and some could be 2 to 3 feet (0.6 to 0.9 meters) wide. In 1906, De Forest took a British invention called the Fleming Tube—developed by an English electrical engineer named Sir John Ambrose Fleming (1849–1945)—and modified it, adding a third small coil to the two already in the Fleming Tube's glass bulb. De Forest called his invention the **audion tube**.

The audion tube (also called the vacuum tube or the triode) replaced large coils of wire, enabling radio

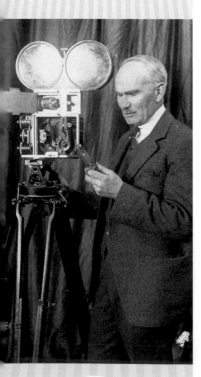

▼ *Dr. Lee De Forest first demonstrated his Phonofilm invention, the first sound-on-film process, in theaters in 1923.*

transmitters and receivers to become smaller. It also greatly amplified the radio signal from the transmitter and increased the sensitivity of radio receivers. Radio signals could now travel over greater distances.

De Forest hoped to become rich and famous with his invention. He also popularized radio with publicity stunts such as **broadcasting** from the top of the Eiffel Tower in Paris, France, in 1908, and broadcasting a concert by the famous singer Enrico Caruso from the Metropolitan Opera House in New York in 1910. This concert is generally believed to be the first scheduled radio broadcast in history. De Forest was one of the first to think of radio as a potential means of communicating from one point or person to many points at the same time.

The vacuum tube became the basis not only for radio and then television, but for radar, sonar, sound in movies, guided missiles, automated machines, long-distance telephone communication, and early computers. It remained the primary heart of electronics until the invention of the **transistor** in the late 1940s, which replaced the vacuum tube in most electronic equipment. De Forest's invention led to the spread of radio transmission as a hobby. Hundreds of amateur, or "ham," radio operators began searching the night skies for radio waves from far away.

Armstrong Ups the Stakes

American inventor and engineer Edwin Howard Armstrong (1890–1954) had far greater technical knowledge than De Forest. Armstrong, an amateur wireless operator, set out to discover just how the De Forest audion tube worked (something that De Forest himself was never certain of), so he could increase its power and amplify its signal.

Reginald Fessenden (1866–1932)

Although Lee De Forest often claimed to be the first person to broadcast the human voice over radio waves, he was in fact beaten to this achievement by Reginald Fessenden, a professor at the University of Pittsburgh in Pennsylvania. In December 1900, Fessenden broadcast a weak, poor-quality signal carrying a human voice over a distance of 1 mile (1.6 km). Six years later, on Christmas Eve 1906, Fessenden made what is considered to be the first good-quality radio broadcast. That night, wireless operators 15 miles (24 km) out to sea, used to hearing the beeps and blips of radio telegraphy, were surprised to hear music and a voice come through their headphones. Fessenden himself played "O Holy Night" on the violin and read from the Bible at his transmitter in Brant Rock, Massachusetts.

By feeding the audion tube's signal back into itself up to twenty thousand times per second, Armstrong achieved a huge increase in signal strength, which he called regeneration. This discovery in 1912 was one of the most significant advances in the technical history of radio. Armstrong's invention, which he patented in 1913, made the transmission of voice and music much clearer. Radio signals could now travel greater distances than they ever had.

Armstrong would add two more great inventions to radio's development. In 1917, while in the army during World War I (1914–1918), he created the **superheterodyne** radio receiver. Before this invention, many adjustments had to be made to find a particular radio frequency. Now, one dial could be turned to move from frequency to frequency (eventually, from radio station to radio station). This device also became the basis for tuning in different stations on television and satellite systems.

Armstrong's final contribution to radio was the production of FM (frequency modulation) waves. These were radio waves that delivered high-quality sound with no static. Signals on AM (amplitude modulation), the type of radio waves that were originally used, presented limited sound quality and were filled with static. FM would eventually become the choice of radio stations (and listeners) for broadcasting music and would be the type of radio waves used to broadcast sound on television.

After Armstrong patented his first great break-through—regeneration—in 1913, he showed his invention to the chief inspector of the American Marconi Company, David Sarnoff (1891–1971). Sarnoff suggested that Armstrong license his discovery to the Marconi Company. Armstrong agreed. The meeting of these two men led to a huge leap forward in the development of radio as it is known today.

MORE THAN A WIRELESS TELEGRAPH

David Sarnoff had no hand in any of the technical inventions that brought radio into existence. More than any other individual, however, he was responsible for radio becoming the medium for mass communication that it evolved into in the 1920s. Sarnoff was a business leader and a visionary who envisioned a radio informing and entertaining people in every home in the country. Sarnoff, a Russian immigrant, rose from poverty to become president of the most powerful communications company in the United States, the Radio Corporation of America (RCA). He began his meteoric rise as a telegraph operator for the American Marconi Company.

On April 14, 1912, while Sarnoff was on duty, he picked up a wireless telegraph message that the brand-new ocean liner, the S.S. *Titanic*, had struck an iceberg and was sinking in the freezing cold Atlantic Ocean. Although more than one thousand people died in the disaster, more than seven hundred were rescued, thanks to the wireless message sent by Sarnoff to a nearby ship equipped with a Marconi wireless system.

Following the *Titanic* tragedy, federal laws were passed forcing all large oceangoing ships to carry wireless equipment. Sarnoff, however, viewed wireless transmission (soon to be called *radio*) as more than simply a means of emergency communications.

▼ *David Sarnoff was a business executive who believed in the potential of radio and the role it would play in the everyday lives of Americans.*

Never Forgot

Years after the higher-ups at the American Marconi Company refused to discuss Sarnoff's memo presenting his vision of radio as a "household utility," Sarnoff, who had risen to the top of RCA, enjoyed taking out the yellowed document and showing people that he had been right—and first!

▼ *American inventor Emile Berliner experiments with an early microphone and a more contemporary design to illustrate its development. Berliner's research and advances in the areas of sound and recording were vital to many industries and institutions.*

In 1915, in a now-famous memo to his bosses at the American Marconi Company, Sarnoff wrote: "I have in mind a plan of development which would make radio a 'household utility' in the same sense as the piano or phonograph [the two main forms of home entertainment at that time]. The idea is to bring music into the home by wireless." His bosses didn't even bother to reply to the memo, but Sarnoff continued to pursue his vision of a radio music box.

Word War I and Beyond

World War I was the first war in which radio played a role. With radio, commanders could receive reports from soldiers in the field, and government officials could communicate with other officials across a continent or an ocean. The war also pushed radio technology research into high gear. All work on the development of radio as a commercial mass medium stopped in favor of using the invention for the war effort. Technological advances made during the war, such as Armstrong's superheterodyne radio receiver, would be applied to the growing industry after the fighting stopped.

After the war, American leaders in Washington, D.C., worried that American radio was controlled by a foreign company, the British Marconi Company, through its American subsidiary, the American Marconi Company. Also, the patents for many of the great inventions making radio possible were scattered among several companies. This held back the growth of radio, since no single company could manufacture radio equipment without infringing on patents held by others.

To remedy this situation, in 1919, under pressure from the U.S. government, the American Marconi

Company formed RCA. This new company acquired the assets and patents of the American Marconi Company, which included Armstrong's patents. It also arranged to share many of De Forest's patents, which were held by the electronic companies General Electric (GE), Westinghouse, and American Telephone & Telegraph (AT&T).

By the end of 1920, RCA had set up commercial wireless telegraph service between the United States and England, France, Germany, Norway, Hawaii, and Japan. In addition to its telegraph business, RCA held patents for both the equipment to transmit radio signals and the electronics needed to manufacture radio receivers. Twenty-eight-year-old David Sarnoff was named general manager of the new company. By the following year, Sarnoff's dream of the radio as a household utility was about to come true.

Early Broadcasting

Radio stations sprang up around the country in the early 1920s. Early broadcasters were amateurs, sending their signals out to those few people who had radio receivers. A Westinghouse engineer named Frank Conrad (1874–1941)—a "hobbyist," as early amateur radio enthusiasts were called— began broadcasting in 1919 from his garage near Pittsburgh. Conrad played records on the air that had been donated by a local record store. The owner of the store noticed that sales of the records that Conrad played increased.

In September 1920, a Pittsburgh department store mentioned Conrad's broadcasts in an ad for radio receivers the store was selling.

▼ Frank Conrad, an engineer by trade, first broadcast music to listeners from his garage. This 1924 picture shows him with his earliest transmitter.

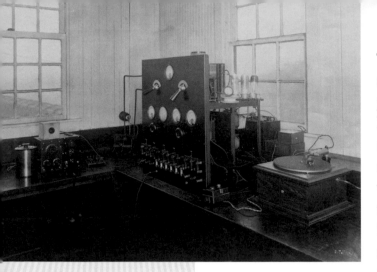

▲ *The Westinghouse Company provided Frank Conrad with this transmitter and studio, launching the first commercial broadcast station in America.*

The store's supply of radios sold out instantly. A vice president at Westinghouse, Harry P. Davis, saw the ad. He decided to set Conrad up with a more powerful transmitter, which was placed on top of the Westinghouse plant in Pittsburgh, along with a brand-new radio studio. Then he put some of Westinghouse's production plants back to work. These plants had increased their production capability during World War I but had remained idle since the end of the war. Now, instead of military equipment, they would manufacture radios.

Conrad and Davis applied to the U.S. government and received the first commercial broadcast license in the United States. The new, more powerful station went on the air as KDKA, Pittsburgh, on November 2, 1920. Its first broadcast covered the results of the presidential election between Warren G. Harding and James Cox. Only five hundred to one thousand radios received this initial broadcast, but the coverage was given widespread publicity.

Within weeks, Westinghouse capitalized on the excitement generated by KDKA and began setting up radio stations with powerful transmitters in Newark, New Jersey (WJZ), Springfield, Massachusetts (WBZ), and Chicago, Illinois (KYW). These stations began broadcasting regularly scheduled programs announced in advance. By the end of 1921, twenty-eight radio stations had been given licenses to broadcast. One year later, the number was closer to five hundred. By 1924, close to fifteen hundred radio stations were licensed around the United States.

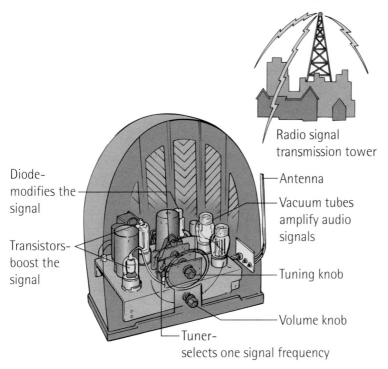

Radio signal transmission tower

Diode- modifies the signal

Transistors- boost the signal

Antenna

Vacuum tubes amplify audio signals

Tuning knob

Volume knob

Tuner- selects one signal frequency

◄ *A radio has two parts, the transmitter and the receiver. The transmitter is usually located at the base of a tower. The transmitter takes some sort of message (it could be music or a person's voice), encodes it into an electromagnetic wave, and transmits it as radio waves. The receiver, which can be located anywhere in a car, or a house, or an office building, receives the radio waves and decodes the message from the electromagnetic wave transmitted. Both the transmitter and the receiver use antennas to radiate and capture the radio signal. The radio shown in this diagram is an early model that needed a minute or so to "warm up" vacuum tubes that amplify the incoming signal.*

The First Network

While RCA was busy distributing and marketing radio receivers built by Westinghouse and GE, Westinghouse was establishing itself as a leader in the new field of broadcasting. David Sarnoff's vision of radio as a music box for the home was being realized—but not by his company.

Inspired by this competition, Sarnoff dusted off his 1915 memo to show his bosses at RCA that he had seen this coming and that RCA, not Westinghouse, should be the leader in the world of broadcasting. This time, they agreed to back Sarnoff financially. Sarnoff wanted to make a big splash by covering a major event, similar to KDKA's coverage of the 1920 presidential election. On July 2, 1921, heavyweight boxing champion Jack Dempsey was to fight a French boxer named Georges Carpentier in one of the biggest sporting events of the decade. Sarnoff decided that RCA would broadcast the fight.

▲ By 1930, baseball games were regularly broadcast over the airwaves, spawning new careers for sports journalists. In this photograph, sportscaster Graham McNamee interviews world-famous baseball player Babe Ruth during a New York Yankee game. Hundreds of thousands of radio listeners were eager to listen to the words of one of the game's most beloved players.

Sarnoff borrowed a large transmitter, which he set up near the boxing arena in Jersey City, New Jersey. He then sent an announcer to cover the fight. Remote broadcasting technology, of the kind that allows sports events to be covered around the world today, did not exist in 1921. So an announcer relayed the blow-by-blow description via a telephone to an RCA technician at the transmitter. The technician then repeated the description into a microphone attached to the transmitter, which then broadcast it to the New York City area. More than 300,000 people heard the broadcast. For the first time in history, people listening at home learned the details of a major sporting event as they happened, rather than reading about them in the next day's newspaper. The audience was thrilled and amazed by the miracle of broadcasting.

In the fall of 1921, the Westinghouse station WJZ broadcast a pitch-by-pitch account of the World Series. One person at the ballpark relayed the details over the telephone to an announcer at the station, who then shared them with the radio audience.

In 1922, David Sarnoff wrote another memo to his bosses. This time, he outlined his belief that the future growth of radio in the United States would not be found in small, individual local stations, but rather in linking stations across the country together into a national network. He explained that this radio network would "entertain a nation" with music, news, sports, plays, and other cultural events heard by millions across the country **simultaneously**.

By 1926, after years of negotiation and deal making, Sarnoff's envisioned network became reality. In a deal that would transform broadcasting, RCA agreed to rent telephone lines from AT&T, using them to link its stations together into a national network. A new company, called the National Broadcasting Company (NBC) was formed, composed of two networks—the NBC Red Network and the NBC Blue Network. Both were subsidiaries of RCA.

Other companies would follow Sarnoff's lead. In 1928, the Columbia Broadcasting System (CBS) was formed under the guidance of William S. Paley (1901–1990). Then in 1943, the Federal Communications Commission (FCC) grew concerned with the concentration of broadcasting power held by only a few companies. Under FCC pressure, NBC sold its Blue Network to Edward Noble (1882–1958), and the American Broadcasting Company (ABC) was formed.

On June 27, 1927, Charles Lindbergh returned to the United States aboard an ocean liner after his historic first solo, nonstop transatlantic flight to Paris. NBC linked together fifty radio stations in twenty-four states to cover the event. More than 30 million people across the country listened. Sarnoff's latest dream had come true. The Golden Age of Radio was about to begin.

The Federal Communications Commission

The FCC is an independent U.S. government agency directly responsible to Congress. The FCC was established by the Communications Act of 1934 to regulate interstate and international communications by radio and wire. It assigns broadcast licenses and frequencies to broadcasters so that the radio dial doesn't get too crowded. The FCC also regulates ownership of stations and use of "indecent" language on the air. As new technologies emerged, television, satellite, and cable were added to its list of responsibilities. The FCC's jurisdiction covers the United States and U.S. possessions.

4 THE GOLDEN AGE OF RADIO

▼ *William S. Paley revolutionized the broadcasting industry by linking different radio stations together to share programming and business costs.*

As radio stations, networks, and receivers spread throughout the United States, the new medium of radio had a profound impact on American society. In the years before radio, life in small-town America was made up of local activities. For entertainment, people played the piano in their own homes. They gathered on neighbors' porches to exchange local news or gossip. Social activities included picnics and band concerts in a local park.

Occasionally, a traveling theater group or circus would come to town to perform. Perhaps once or twice a year, a family might travel to the nearest big city for a visit, to glimpse life in another place. Local newspapers, using the national wire services that transmitted news over telegraph lines, would bring some news of the world outside the little towns or even outside the United States. This was limited, however, and often not up to date. General-interest magazines like the *Saturday Evening Post* provided weekly entertainment, bringing a variety of events into the homes of rural Americans.

The growth of radio broadcasting brought an end to the isolation of small-town America. Music, news, Shakespearean plays, and major sporting events came into homes from far away, opening a door beyond the boundaries of the immediate community.

The radio informed and entertained people, and eventually, it sold them products they didn't even know existed. For the first time in history, one speaker could spread information, entertainment, propaganda, political points of view, religious fervor, cultural ideas, and even hatred and intolerance to millions simultaneously.

Early Radio Programs

Early radio programs borrowed the talent and program structure of existing forms of entertainment and culture. Singers and comedians from the vaudeville stage brought their talents into radio studios for broadcasting around the country. In fact, radio is often credited with "killing" vaudeville.

Before radio, vaudeville performers traveled from town to town around the country, doing their "act," a set series of songs (for singers) or jokes (for comedians), in theaters. As radio increased in popularity,

Vaudeville

In the late 1800s and early 1900s, vaudeville grew to enormous popularity in the United States. Vaudeville was devised as inexpensive theater for a growing middle class that enjoyed more and more leisure time. Vaudeville companies were composed of a variety of entertainers. Singers, dancers, comedians, acrobats, jugglers, and other circus and carnival acts toured the country, performing in theaters specifically dedicated to this type of entertainment. Vaudeville marked the beginning of popular entertainment as big business. The radio, television, film, and music industries followed the model established by this now-lost art form.

▲ *The Andrews Sisters, a singing group made up of three sisters from Minneapolis, Minnesota, found great success with the growth of radio and later went on to film and stage careers.*

people all over the country could now hear these acts at home. There was no need to wait months or years for those performers to reach town.

This change also led to the need for a lot more material. Before radio, a comedian could travel around the country doing the same set of jokes in city after city. But a comedian who appeared on the air one week couldn't simply come back the next week and tell the same jokes, since the audience had already heard them. Radio thus created a great need for writers, who were hired to produce new material daily.

Opera singers, jazz musicians, and classical musicians all performed on the air. Radio dramas soon became popular. These programs ranged from tales of the Old West *(The Lone Ranger)* to futuristic science fiction *(Buck Rogers in the Twenty-Fifth Century)* to adventure programs featuring great heroes *(The Green Hornet, The Shadow,* and *Superman).*

Radio comedians such as Jack Benny, Fred Allen, Bob Hope, Eddie Cantor, and George Burns and Gracie Allen became enormously popular. Many would go on to even greater success in films and television. The situation comedy (or sitcom), now a staple of television programming, began on radio with such shows as *Fibber McGee and Molly, Duffy's Tavern,* and *Our Miss Brooks.* The same was true of the ongoing dramas that were called soap operas because they were sponsored by soap manufacturing companies. *The Guiding Light,* for example, began as a radio soap opera, then continued its long run on television.

By far, the most successful early radio program was *Amos 'n' Andy.* The program consisted of two white performers, Freeman Gosden and Charles

Correll, playing black characters. They told stories and acted out humorous situations with a recurring cast of characters. The racial stereotypes reinforced on the program would be considered offensive and unacceptable by today's social standards. In 1929, however, when the show was broadcast on the NBC network, it became an instant hit.

For the next three years, more than half the radios in the United States were tuned to *Amos 'n' Andy* each weeknight from seven o'clock to seven fifteen. Factories changed shift hours so that workers could hear the program. Restaurants closed during that quarter hour, because they had no customers. Even movies piped the program through their speaker systems so that people wouldn't stay home in order to hear the show.

The phenomenon of a shared common experience that came right into people's homes was something brand-new in American life. Stories had been **serialized** in magazines. Movie serials had people going back to movie theaters week after week. Newspaper comic strip adventures had readers anxiously awaiting the next installment. Nothing in the history of entertainment and storytelling, however, equaled the popularity or impact of the fresh material that arrived, seemingly by magic, in people's living rooms, night after night.

Fast Fact

Freeman Gosden and Charles Correll, who portrayed Amos and Andy, met in 1920 and began doing a vaudeville act in blackface (makeup used to make white actors look black) with music, dancing, and storytelling. In 1928, this act was put on a radio station in Chicago, and it eventually evolved into the *Amos 'n' Andy* radio program.

Live from New York!

In the early years of radio broadcasting, there was much more airtime to fill than there were programs to fill it. One announcer, stuck for an idea, simply opened the window of his Manhattan radio studio and said to his nationwide audience, "Ladies and gentlemen, the sounds of New York City." Then he stuck his microphone out the window. People in faraway towns, who might never have the chance to visit New York, loved it. There, in their homes, was the hustle and bustle of the busiest U.S. city!

▲ President Roosevelt's weekly radio speeches, known as fireside chats, reassured a worried nation throughout the Great Depression and then World War II.

The Great Depression

In March 1933, the U.S. banking system came close to collapsing. Four years into the national economic despair known as the Great Depression, the fiscal crisis triggered by the 1929 stock market crash reached its lowest point. Worried that what money they had would become worthless, people rushed to the banks to withdraw whatever was left. This run on the banks, if allowed to continue, could have resulted in the collapse of the U.S. economy. On Friday, March 10, 1993, President Franklin Delano Roosevelt ordered the banks closed.

On Sunday evening, March 12, the president asked for radio time to talk to the American people about the worsening economic crisis. He spoke calmly and reassuringly about the need for all Americans to work together to get through this time of national hardship. He discussed federal programs that would be created to help struggling Americans survive.

Roosevelt's radio chat helped calm people's fears. This radio address marked the first time in history that a president—indeed any politician—had reached millions of Americans at once. President Roosevelt decided to use radio to address the nation regularly.

Roosevelt's weekly radio addresses also changed American politics. Now politicians—both those already in office and those campaigning to win an election—could speak to millions of voters at once. Before radio, politicians had to travel around the country, usually by train, holding rallies and making speeches every time the train stopped.

During these times, radio also brought escape from the grim reality of life—something Americans desperately sought. For a few hours each night, through radio dramas, people could lose themselves in the past or on a distant planet. They could chuckle at the antics of their favorite comedians or be soothed by beautiful music. Radio had become a valued friend, always there to keep one company.

World War II

On December 7, 1941, as World War II (1939–1945) raged in Europe, the Japanese bombed the American naval fleet at Pearl Harbor in Hawaii. The news poured out of radio receivers, spreading rapidly across the country. Within hours, President Roosevelt was on the air, once again addressing the nation in a time of crisis.

Roosevelt announced that the United States had declared war on Japan and its ally, Germany, formally entering World War II. For the next four years, as millions of American soldiers fought around the world, radio reports kept those left behind informed about the conflict.

As the war progressed, Americans counted on radio to bring them the latest news, weekly chats from the president, and entertaining distractions from worries about loved ones overseas. Radio journalists filed reports from warships, battlefields, and the barracks where soldiers were stationed, bringing the war home. In 1945, it was radio that informed Americans that the war was over.

The period known as the Golden Age of Radio lasted from the late 1920s until the early 1950s. Radio had become such a vital part of everyday American life that people couldn't imagine living without it. Just as the medium achieved its greatest success, however, a new invention came along that would transform the way Americans used their radios.

5 RADIO WITH PICTURES

At the 1939 World's Fair in New York, in front of the RCA Pavilion (which was shaped like a giant radio tube), David Sarnoff introduced a new invention that would revolutionize broadcasting. As he had predicted twenty years earlier about radio, Sarnoff announced that television would soon be in every American home, providing entertainment and information not just through sound, but with pictures, as well.

The idea for television went back to the late 1800s. Two different types of systems for sending a picture to a receiver were developed—mechanical television and electronic television.

▼ The first television news broadcast covered the dedication of the RCA Pavilion by David Sarnoff at the 1939 World's Fair.

Spinning Discs and Glowing Tubes

The road to television began in Germany in 1883, when a research student named Paul Nipkow (1860–1940) created a scanning device to capture an image. This was the first example of a mechanical television system. For television to work, an image would have to be captured (scanned) and converted into electrical signals. The Nipkow disc, as his invention came to be called, was a circular disc with small holes that began in the center and spiraled out toward the edge. As the disc revolved, each hole passed over a section of an image, exposing it to light. The light was then turned into electrical current. This current was sent to an identical disc spinning on the other end of the signal. Here, the electric current was changed back into light, and the image was re-created by the second spinning disc.

In 1897, German physicist Karl Braun (1850–1918) added a fluorescent screen to one end of a tube through which electricity was passing, creating the **cathode-ray tube**. This would become the basis for television screens as they are known today. When a beam of electricity in the tube hit the fluorescent screen, the screen would glow with visible light. Television had taken its first step away from being a mechanical device to becoming an electronic one.

The next step in that journey was taken in 1907. Russian physicist Boris Rosing (1869–1933) replaced

Lines of Resolution

A television picture is made up of lines called *lines of resolution*. The more lines that are used, the clearer the picture is. A standard television set uses 525 lines. Farnsworth achieved 60 lines in 1927. Today's high-definition systems generate well over 1,000 lines of resolution.

Vladimir Zworykin (1889–1982)

Vladimir Zworykin studied electrical engineering at Petrograd (present-day St. Petersburg), Russia, graduating in 1912. During World War I, he served as a radio officer in the Russian army. Moving to the United States in 1919, he joined the Westinghouse Electric Corporation the following year. He received a Ph.D. in 1926 from University of Pittsburgh and then joined RCA in 1929. There, David Sarnoff put Zworykin's talents to work, helping the company become the leader in the development of television.

the receiving disc in the Nipkow system with Braun's cathode-ray tube. The image was still scanned mechanically by a Nipkow disc and converted into an electronic signal. For the first time, however, that signal was re-created by the receiver not mechanically, but electronically, using the cathode-ray tube.

In 1908, Scottish engineer Campbell Swinton (1863–1930) took Rosing's idea one step further. He published a detailed proposal for a completely electronic television system, using cathode-ray tubes at both ends of the system—inside the TV camera and in the receiver. His ideas formed the basis for modern TV broadcasting.

Swinton's theories were put into practice in 1923 by a student of Rosing's named Vladimir Zworykin (1889–1982). Zworykin, a Russian-born American engineer, invented the **iconoscope**, or camera tube. The iconoscope became the heart of the television camera, just as the cathode-ray tube was the heart of the television receiver. This achievement did not go unnoticed by David Sarnoff, who was convinced that television would become even more popular than radio. Sarnoff hired Zworykin to bring television to RCA.

In 1927, while Zworykin and others were developing television systems, an obscure, twenty-year-old inventor, working independently, filed a patent for an all-electronic television system. Philo Farnsworth created a system that vastly improved picture quality. Working in relative obscurity and with little outside backing, Farnsworth competed against the giant RCA—which backed Vladimir Zworykin with a lot of money and teams of engineers—to get the first commercially viable TV system on the air. After years of patent suits and legal wrangling, Farnsworth was eventually worn out by Sarnoff's unlimited resources at RCA, and after he died, he became only a footnote in the story of the invention of television. Still, many historians consider Philo Farnsworth the true "father of TV."

Early Broadcasts

Three years before David Sarnoff formally introduced television to the world at the 1939 World's Fair, Sarnoff's NBC opened its first broadcast studio dedicated exclusively to television. For three years before that, NBC technicians had labored to convert a radio studio into a fully operational TV facility. Studio 3H in Rockefeller Center was only 20 feet by 50 feet (6.1 m by 15.2 m) and had low ceilings. The movements of the big, bulky television cameras were very limited in this cramped space, and the extremely powerful lights needed to create an image were very hot. Everyone involved in this infant medium—engineers, technicians, performers, and producers—spent most of the time improvising solutions for what seemed to be nonstop technical problems. The first broadcast from NBC's Studio 3H, in 1936, featured cabaret singer Hildegarde, radio comedian Ed Wynn, and dancers from the Radio City Rockettes. Despite poor picture quality, and the fact that only about 150 homes had television receivers that year, Sarnoff declared the broadcast a success.

Also in 1936, William Paley of the CBS radio network, which was lagging behind in the development of television, bought a television broadcasting system from RCA. He set up studios in New York City's Chrysler Building, near the CBS radio facilities. CBS would not begin regular TV broadcasts until after World War II.

That same year in England, the British Broadcasting Corporation (BBC) broadcast the

Fast Fact

Too Hot!

A tremendous amount of light—1,000 **foot-candles** (10,760 meter-candles)—was needed to produce images using early TV cameras. That much light gave off an intense amount of heat, causing the temperature in TV studios to soar and performers to sweat—or even faint!

world's first regularly scheduled television programs from Alexandra Palace in London. BBC also broadcast the first out-of-studio (remote) events, including the 1936 Olympics in Berlin, Germany, and the coronation of King George VI of England in 1937.

The first major remote broadcast in the United States was Sarnoff's famous introduction of this great new invention at the RCA Pavilion at the 1939 World's Fair. This broadcast included an opening address by President Roosevelt. That same year, a game between the Brooklyn Dodgers and the Cincinnati Reds became the first baseball game ever televised.

The First Network, the First Station

In 1940, RCA created an invention that led to two major developments in television. The **coaxial cable**—a thick cable made up of smaller cables wrapped around each other—could carry a television signal great distances without loss of picture quality. This breakthrough led to the creation of the first

▼ In 1936, the Philco Radio and Television Corporation demonstrated this early television model.

Radio and Television

The First Politician on TV

During the 1920s, many scientists experimented with mechanical television systems. At Bell Laboratories, Herbert Ives (1882–1953) led a team that developed a working mechanical TV. During the 1928 election, Ives convinced Herbert Hoover, who was running for president, to appear on his system, although almost no one had the devices needed to receive the broadcast. Hoover agreed and became the first politician to appear on television.

television network. It also made the transmission of TV signals in color possible.

Early in 1940, an NBC program being broadcast in New York City was also seen by viewers in Schenectady, New York. The signal was carried on coaxial cable. Later that year, events from the Republican National Convention in Philadelphia, Pennsylvania, and the Democratic National Convention in Chicago were seen on television by viewers in New York. Experimental color broadcasts began in the 1940s, but color TV would not become practical and popular until the 1960s.

In 1940, RCA sold black-and-white television sets that had 10-inch (25-centimeter) screens. People who purchased televisions sent a postcard to RCA to let the company know that they were now viewers. In return, RCA sent back a notice listing the programming that would appear each week on its experimental station, known as W2XBS. The programs included a fifteen-minute newscast at 6:45 each evening, which was actually a television broadcast of a radio announcer doing his radio newscast. At the time, there were about 2,500 television sets in the New York area. This meant that while a few thousand people were watching the newscast, 100 million were listening to it over the radio.

Fast Fact

RCA sold its small black-and-white TV set for about $395 in 1940. This was more than a month's salary for most Americans at that time.

One Candle

In 1948, RCA invited engineers and executives of the young television industry to Madison Square Garden for a demonstration of Vladimir Zworykin's new invention, the image-orthicon tube. The crowd gathered around a television screen on one side of the large arena. On the other side of the arena, in bright lights, sat a man on a horse in front of a television camera, which contained an image-orthicon tube. Suddenly every light in the building was turned off, plunging the cavernous arena into total darkness. The man on the horse then struck a match and lit a single candle. To the amazement of all, the man and the horse, lit solely by the power of one candle, were clearly visible on the TV screen. Zworykin's invention changed the way television shows could be lit from that point forward.

W2XBS also showed short films and films from minor studios; the major film studios did not want their movies to be shown on the home screen for free. Sporting events, like college basketball games from Madison Square Garden, were also shown, as were early quiz shows. The quiz show was a popular format taken from radio.

The arrival of a television set in a home also meant the arrival of curious neighbors who wanted to watch popular shows. Stores that sold televisions often placed sets in their windows, attracting crowds of people who gathered on the sidewalks in front of the stores to watch programs.

In addition to RCA, other companies such as DuMont, Philco, and Zenith began manufacturing television receivers. The systems were not **compatible**, however—each had a different number of lines of resolution, so not every set could pick up every broadcast. Because of this incompatibility, the FCC had refused to issue any commercial television licenses. Early in 1941, David Sarnoff, using RCA's money and influence, convinced the other manufacturers to use the RCA system (525 lines of resolution). On July 1, 1941, the FCC granted a license to RCA. Experimental station W2XBS became WNBT, the first fully licensed television station with the right to broadcast advertising in order to pay for its programming.

World War II

When the United States entered World War II in December 1941, the development of television slowed down greatly. The Defense Department ordered an end to the construction of new television stations. Existing stations were used in the war effort for such purposes as civil defense and air-raid training messages, Red Cross instructions, and war bond sales. The best technical minds in television were turned to the technology of war, and the young medium had to wait for the conflict to end.

After the war, efforts to mass-produce television sets and to make commercial television a reality went into full gear. As networks grew, the amount of programming increased. More programs led to more people buying televisions, and the purchase of more sets led to the demand for even more programming. This cycle of growth would soon make television popular and widespread. Screens (some rounded, some rectangular) got larger, up to 20 inches (51 cm) in the late 1940s, and the images got better, thanks mostly to another new invention.

In 1948, Vladimir Zworykin, still working for RCA, unveiled his second great invention, the **image-orthicon tube**. This tube, to be used in TV cameras, was extremely sensitive to light and eliminated the need for the intense amount of light previously necessary to send a quality picture.

▼ Early color television sets came in unusual shapes that little resembled the TVs of today. This particular RCA model had 22 percent more picture area than any other color television yet produced at the time.

The FCC also decided that FM, invented in 1935 by Edwin Armstrong, would be used for all television sound. Its superior sound quality and lack of static made it an obvious choice. FM use in radio, however, would not become popular until the 1960s.

At the end of 1941, there were several thousand TV sets in the United States. By the end of 1948, there were more than 1 million. Many historians credit one man with the explosion of television's popularity—a former vaudeville and radio comedian named Milton Berle (1908–2002).

Uncle Miltie

On Tuesday nights beginning in 1948, every television set in the United States was tuned into *Texaco Star Theater*, a variety show starring Milton Berle. As with the *Amos 'n' Andy* radio show twenty years earlier, people planned their schedules around the program. Friends and neighbors gathered at the homes of those who owned TV sets so as not to miss the zany antics of the man who soon became known as "Uncle Miltie" and later earned the nickname "Mr. Television." City streets were empty and movie theaters closed on Tuesday nights, because they simply couldn't compete. One movie house manager even placed a sign on the door of his closed theater that read: "Closed Tuesday—I want to see Berle, too!" Television was well on its way to becoming an integral part of everyday life in the country.

▼ As more and more people bought televisions, programming increased, bringing all types of entertainment into the home. Comedians Bob Hope and Milton Berle were especially popular with Americans. In this 1978 photograph, they are reminiscing about the early days of broadcasting for a CBS network special.

Radio and Television

In 1948, there were thirty-six television stations on the air in the United States, another seventy or so under construction, and about 1 million TV sets in use. Programs were carried by four networks. NBC, under David Sarnoff's leadership, had created the concept of the television network (many stations around the country all broadcasting the same programs). CBS was run by William S. Paley, who felt that quality programming was what would attract viewers. ABC, the network that had originally been the NBC Blue Radio Network, now also ventured into television broadcasting. Lastly, the DuMont Network was set up by the DuMont Company—RCA's biggest competitor in the manufacture and sale of television sets. The DuMont Network lasted only until 1955. The other three still exist today.

In the early days of television networks, most of the stations were concentrated in a few big cities like Boston, Massachusetts; Los Angeles, California; and New York, Chicago, and Philadelphia. As more coaxial cable was installed and the FCC

▼ As television sets became commonplace in people's homes, the networks expanded their programming. I Love Lucy became an instant hit when audiences laughed along with Lucille Ball (left) and Desi Arnaz (right), the married stars of the show.

established regulations guiding the development
and placement of new stations, many more stations
sprang up all over the country. By 1949, there were
close to 400 stations across the United States. By
1954, 90 percent of the country had television
coverage, and more than half of homes had a TV
set. As the number of sets grew and programming
expanded, television rapidly replaced radio as the
dominant medium for information and entertainment
in the home.

Widespread Phenomenon, Shared Moments

In the 1950s, for the first time, people all across the
United States shared important moments with each
other through television. During
the decade, events were shaped
to fit on television, not simply
photographed by its cameras.
The 1952 presidential campaign
between Dwight Eisenhower and
Adlai Stevenson was the first
presidential campaign to be waged
on television. The Eisenhower campaign hired an advertising agency
to create short "announcements"—
the first TV campaign ads—that
ran about twenty seconds long.
These announcements presented
images of Eisenhower, who had
been a general in World War II,
as a war hero and a great leader.
He easily won the election.

The president considered the
first "television president" was

Radio and Television

John F. Kennedy. His 1960 presidential debate with rival Richard M. Nixon first made Americans aware of the power of television to influence lives. Young, handsome, and composed, Kennedy came across brilliantly in the televised debate. Nixon, a far more experienced politician, sweated profusely under the lights, and his facial mannerisms led people to view him as nervous. Most of those who watched the debate on TV believed that Kennedy had won. However, those who listened to the very same debate on the radio believed that Nixon had won, clearly demonstrating the power of the picture. Kennedy won the election by the narrowest of margins.

Three years later, the nation mourned Kennedy's death together through television. After the assassination of President Kennedy, Americans stayed glued to their televisions for four days, watching the continuous coverage leading up to his funeral. This included the murder on live TV of his accused assassin, Lee Harvey Oswald. Because of television, the nation could grieve as one big family. Since then, Americans have frequently turned to television for information and comfort during times of national tragedy, such as during the *Challenger* and *Columbia* space shuttle disasters and the terrorist attacks of September 11, 2001.

Television has also been there during times of great achievement. When Neil Armstrong and Edwin "Buzz" Aldrin landed on the Moon in 1969, the world watched on television. The astronauts sent back live images from the Moon's surface, including amazing views of Earth in space. This event demonstrated clearly the potential of the medium beyond its ability to simply entertain.

If John Kennedy was the first "television president," then the Vietnam War (1959–1975) was the first

William S. Paley (1901–1990)

If David Sarnoff was known as the visionary of television broadcasting, recognizing the potential of the medium, then William S. Paley was its programming genius. Paley recognized that TV's novelty would quickly wear off and that quality programming was required to keep people coming back. Born in Chicago, the son of a successful cigar merchant, Paley bought the CBS radio network in 1929 for $400,000 and turned it into a broadcasting empire. When TV came along, he got quality programming from dramas like *Studio One*, comedic talent like Lucille Ball, Jack Benny, and Jackie Gleason, journalists like Edward R. Murrow and Walter Cronkite, early children's shows like *Mr. I. Magination*, and the hugely successful variety show hosted by Ed Sullivan.

► *Electronic information is transmitted through wires, cables, or electromagnetic waves from a television station to an antenna on top of a tower located within a given broadcast area. This large antenna sends electromagnetic waves of energy to the smaller antenna attached to the receiver, or TV, in your home. The picture tube within your TV decodes this information into sound and picture parts. The picture tube is the heart of the television. Within the tube are red, blue, and green electron guns. These guns shoot electron beams containing the sound and picture signals from one end of the picture tube to a metal plate with thousands of holes at the other end. The electron beams travel through the holes and fall onto a screen that is coated with strips of colored phosphors, a material that, when exposed to the energy from the electron beams, emits light and makes the screen glow, and a picture comes to life. The TV shown in this diagram receives its signal over the "air," rather than through a cable or via satellite.*

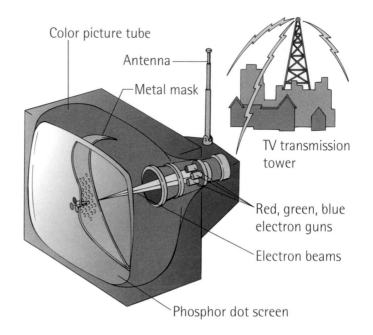

Color picture tube
Antenna
Metal mask
TV transmission tower
Red, green, blue electron guns
Electron beams
Phosphor dot screen

"television war." For the first time in history, images from a conflict in a faraway land appeared in the nation's living rooms each night on the evening news. Many credit television with heightening Americans' awareness of—and growing opposition to—the war.

Color TV

Research into color television continued throughout the late 1940s. RCA was at the forefront, but others were also pursuing the goal of bringing color pictures to the home screen. CBS also developed a color system, as did a company called Color Television, Inc. By 1950, all three systems were ready. In 1953, the National Television Systems Committee (NTSC) and the FCC selected the RCA system to become the industry standard for color TV. It has been in place ever since.

Once its system had been adopted, the rest of the industry left RCA and its network, NBC, to develop and promote color television. By 1963, NBC was broadcasting forty hours a week in color, while CBS had very little color programming and ABC had none. In 1966, NBC became the first network to broadcast all of its programs in color. The other networks soon followed suit. In 1960, there were still very few color TVs sold in the United States. By 1972, half of American households had color TVs. By the end of the 1970s, color TV had become the norm.

▲ *This photograph shows the electron guns inside early color televisions, technology that provided the broad range of color seen on the screen.*

Tape, Transistors, and Miniaturization

From 1948 until 1958, just about every television show was broadcast live. In 1956, RCA developed magnetic video recording tape on which a program could be recorded in advance or edited before going out on the air. By 1959, videotape was widely used in the television industry.

In 1948, scientists at Bell Laboratories invented the transistor, a tiny circuit that would eventually replace the vacuum tube in radios and televisions. In 1960, the first all-transistor television was produced by Sony, a little-known Japanese company. This invention would help Sony become one of the biggest electronics companies in the world. The transistor allowed televisions to get smaller and smaller, eventually leading to today's handheld TVs with 2-inch (5-cm) screens. With television now firmly entrenched in the American home and consciousness, technical breakthroughs continued to advance the medium to where it is today.

Fast Fact

Live programs had become so rare by 1975 that when NBC announced that a new show called *Saturday Night* would be broadcast live, it was a novelty for its time. The show is still on the air as *Saturday Night Live*.

7 RADIO AND TV TODAY AND BEYOND

▼ Flat-screen televisions are just one of the many innovations of recent years. A Sony employee displays a new 50-inch (127-cm) flat-screen plasma TV in 2002. The new model features technological advances that create sharp high-quality images for the viewer.

Cable television, so much a part of life today, was first used in 1950 in rural Pennsylvania. The town of Lansford was high in a mountainous region and couldn't receive normal broadcast signals. The town was wired with coaxial cables that brought TV signals directly into the home. Cable TV soon became popular in areas where mountains or tall buildings in big cities prevented clear reception of broadcast signals. By the 1970s, cable companies with more than 3,500 subscribers were required by the FCC to generate original programs. Today, the technology has spawned many new cable-only networks filled with original programming.

With the rapid growth of the U.S. space program in the 1960s came the launching of satellites that orbited Earth. In 1965, *Early Bird,* the first commercial communications satellite, was launched. Today, a television signal from anywhere on the planet can be sent up to a satellite and then broadcast all around the world. The most recent development in satellite broadcasting involves the use of individual satellite dishes that pick up signals from orbiting satellites in space, bringing thousands of channels of programming right into the home.

Home Recording

Videotape has been in use by the television networks since the mid-1950s, but in the mid-1970s, the home videocassette recorder (VCR) was introduced by Sony for consumer use. TV viewers could record their favorite programs for repeated viewing. Users could set the machine's timer to tape a program when they were not home, so they could watch it later (speeding past the commercials, much to the chagrin of advertisers). They could also watch one program while taping another for later viewing. With the popularity of VCRs also came the practice of buying or renting movies on videotape, which gave way to viewing movies on DVD, bringing digital-quality pictures and sound to home viewing.

The next step in the evolution of home recording was the hard-drive recorder, which appeared in the late 1990s. These recorders can store programs on a computer hard drive for later viewing.

Digital and High-Definition

The late 1990s saw two developments that marked the biggest technical changes in television since the

◄ Sony's Web TV, unveiled in 1997, exploited new technology that linked the Internet to the home television screen. In this photograph, a six-year-old boy easily browses a Web site using a TV and wireless keyboard at a Web TV demonstration.

introduction of color TVs—digital television and high-definition television. Digital broadcast systems convert television signals into binary computer code, providing stronger, more reliable signals. Furthermore, digital signals can carry more information, which results in a more detailed, and therefore clearer, picture. Digital broadcasting led to interactive television, in which viewers can choose what they want to watch at any given time from their cable or satellite providers. The ability of digital systems to carry increased amounts of data also allows viewers to access additional information, in the form of text or voice commentary, relating to the programs they are watching. Digital television combined with miniaturization allows for TV aboard airplanes, as well as portable DVD players.

High-definition television (HDTV) is a type of digital television that provides exceptionally sharp picture quality. Whereas the standard TV picture is made up of 525 lines, the high-definition picture is composed of 1,125 lines. HDTV's scanning pattern (called *progressive scanning*) brings greater clarity than traditional scanning (called *interlaced scanning*) because it scans every line, in order, in every frame. Interlaced scanning systems scan every other line, filling in the blank spaces on a second scanning pass. The first use of HDTV was in England in 1998. Regular HDTV broadcasting began in the United States in 1998 and continues to grow in popularity.

In TV receivers, big, flat screens have become popular. Some use rear projection techniques in which a standard cathode-ray tube projects an image onto the back of a large screen. Other projection systems beam an image across a room onto a larger screen, as films are projected in movie theaters. Flat plasma and liquid crystal displays (LCDs) represent a departure from traditional picture tubes and bring to life the vivid images available through digital and high-definition TV.

Computers and Television

The growth of the personal computer, which began in the 1980s, led to a whole new world of uses for television technology. The marriage of television and computers has led to business applications such as **videoconferencing**. Sitting at desktop computers or in a conference room, people in various locations can hold a meeting, seeing each other on their monitors and sharing documents as if they were all in the same room. Videoconferencing is also used by museums to stage virtual field trips for students. Gathered around a video monitor, students can tour great cultural institutions around the world, without ever leaving their classrooms.

Other combinations of television and computers include video games and the Internet. Video games, which feature sharp graphics and interactivity, have become the twenty-first century's most popular form of entertainment, surpassing movies and television. The Internet places a world of information at a computer user's fingertips.

▲ *Massachusetts National Guard Spc. Danny Sullivan of Brockton, Massachusetts, takes advantage of the latest advances in video conference monitoring as he "talks" with his family while on assignment in Iraq. New satellite communication technology continues to improve the quality of video monitoring.*

Television's Other Uses

The technology of television is used for many things besides broadcasting. Security systems in buildings allow one person sitting in front of a group of

The first color television sets from RCA cost $995. That is the equivalent of over $6,000 today. In 1954, $995 would have purchased a car or, in some areas of the country, a small house.

▼ *In 2004, satellite radio is becoming more popular as a standard feature in new cars. This 2002 photograph shows a satellite radio panel beneath a conventional car radio.*

monitors to view what is going on in many rooms, each equipped with a small TV camera. Doctors can insert tiny TV cameras into the human body and view the resulting images on a monitor. This technology allows views of interior areas of the body never before seen—a useful tool for diagnosis and surgery.

From the beginning of space exploration, television has been used to beam back images of distant moons and planets. During the Moon landing in 1969, the world watched live images of astronauts walking on the Moon's surface. Unmanned spacecraft exploring the solar system and beyond use television to send pictures of faraway planets and remote galaxies to scientists on Earth.

Television technology is also used in electron microscopes. These incredibly powerful tools can enlarge the tiniest particles as much as 500,000 times and enable them to be viewed on television screens in laboratories.

Radio Today

After TV stole the role of the main form of popular entertainment during the 1950s, the medium of radio changed. By the late 1950s, music, news, and talk stations had become radio's main forms of programming, and this remains true today. FM radio came into its own in the 1960s. Because of its excellent sound quality and ability to broadcast in stereo, most FM stations programmed music, although talk radio formats have spread over the FM dial recently. The biggest technological change in radio came in the 1990s with the invention of satellite radio, which beams many channels of programming to special receivers in homes and cars for a subscription fee.

Some hobbyists still broadcast on CB (citizen's band) radios, ham radio sets, and **shortwave** radios.

These amateurs still enjoy point-to-point broadcasting. CB radios are especially popular among truck drivers, who pass long hours on the road chatting with other truckers.

Radio and TV Tomorrow

The future of radio and television is wide open. The merging of technologies makes new inventions possible every day. For example, the combination of wireless radio and telephone technologies has led to the cell phone. Small video screens on cell phones have blended TV, computer, and Internet technology into this mix. Wireless Internet blends cable and radio technologies.

As it has been since its invention, the TV screen will continue to be the center of information in the home. Sets will be connected to cable, satellites, or both for the receiving of programs and connected to computers for interactive communications via the Internet, video games, and videophones. It would have been impossible for inventors like Heinrich Hertz and Guglielmo Marconi to imagine the incredible technological and social developments that came from their early work.

Fast Fact

Shortwave Lives

Although the Internet has made instantaneous worldwide communication easily accessible, shortwave radios remain popular with those who are still thrilled by picking up signals traveling through the air from great distances. The appeal of Heinrich Hertz's radio waves still remains strong, even in the digital age.

Science Fiction or Fact?

Creators of science fiction and popular entertainment have long imagined what communications might be like in the future. In the 1930s, the comic strip *Dick Tracy* featured the detective's two-way wrist radio. This wireless voice device presaged today's cell phones. The view screens, communicators, and tricorders used by the crew of the *USS Enterprise* on the *Star Trek* television series were devices that provided scientific data and transmitted video images and voice communications from place to place. The newest cell phones, with video screens and wireless Internet access, are a first step toward making such instruments a reality.

TIMELINE

1844	Samuel F. B. Morse invents the telegraph, linking the world by wire.
1876	Alexander Graham Bell invents the telephone, adding voice communication.
1883	Paul Nipkow invents the Nipkow disc for use in a mechanical TV system.
1888	Heinrich Hertz produces electromagnetic radio waves.
1896	Guglielmo Marconi sends a wireless telegraph message.
1897	Karl Braun invents the cathode-ray tube, the basis for television reception.
1906	Lee De Forest invents the audion tube, the basis for radio reception.
1912	Edwin Howard Armstrong develops regeneration, greatly boosting the power of radio signals.
1915	David Sarnoff writes a memo in which he envisions radio as a "wireless music box" in every American home.
1920	KDKA, the first commercially licensed radio station, goes on the air in Pittsburgh, Pennsylvania.
1923	Vladimir Zworykin invents the iconoscope, the basis for television cameras.
1926	NBC become the first radio network.
1927	Philo Farnsworth invents the first all-electronic television system.
1935	Edwin Armstrong invents FM radio.
1936	The BBC in England broadcasts the first regular schedule of TV programs. NBC opens the first TV-only broadcast studio in the United States.
1939	Sarnoff introduces the world to television at the World's Fair.
1940	Coaxial cable is invented, resulting in NBC's formation of the first television network and the possibility of color TV.
1941	WNBT becomes the first commercially licensed TV station in the United States.
1948	Zworykin invents the image-orthicon tube, enabling TV cameras to pick up images in low light. Milton Berle becomes television's first big star, and sales of TV sets soar so people can watch his show.
1950	The first cable TV broadcasts take place.
1965	The first communication satellite is launched.
1966	NBC becomes the first network to broadcast all its shows in color.
1975	The first home video recorders are sold.
1981	The IBM PC, the first personal computer, is introduced.
1993	The world's first high-definition television (HDTV) broadcast takes place.
1998	Digital television is introduced in England. Regular HDTV broadcasting begins in the United States.

GLOSSARY

audion tube: a glass enclosure containing three small wires that conduct electricity to amplify a radio signal; also called a vacuum tube

broadcasting: sending out radio or television signals to a large area

cathode-ray tube: the part of a television receiver that converts an electronic signal into a picture

coaxial cable: a thick cable made up of smaller cables wrapped around each other, used to transmit TV signals across a network

compatible: able to work well together

electromagnetic waves: waves of electrical energy that travel through the air from one point to another and are capable of carrying radio or television signals

foot-candle: a measure of the amount of light given off by a candle onto a surface 1 foot (0.3 m) away

iconoscope: the part of a television camera that converts a light image into an electronic signal

image-orthicon tube: a device for converting a light image into an electronic signal in a television camera; it requires much less light than the older iconoscope

instantaneously: immediately

litigation: lawsuit or legal action

magnetic field: a force in the air created by electric current

patent: a legal document that prevents people from stealing or making money from another person's idea or invention

receiver: a device that receives and converts a radio or television signal

serialized: presented in sections or chapters

shortwave: describing a type of radio transmission that travels great distances from one point to another

simultaneously: at the same time

superheterodyne: a type of radio receiver that allows listeners to easily change from one station to another

transistor: a device that carries electrical current within a piece of electronic equipment; it took the place of the vacuum tube

transmitter: a device that sends out a radio or television signal

videoconferencing: linking people in many locations using computers and television monitors so that all the people can see and hear each other and share documents

FOR MORE INFORMATION

Books

Hilmes, Michelle and Jason Loviglio. *Radio Reader: Essays in the Cultural History of Radio.* New York: Routledge, 2002.

Hilmes, Michelle and Jason Jacobs. *The Television History Book.* British Film Institute, 2004.

Maltin, Leonard. *The Great American Broadcast.* New York: Dutton (Penguin), 1997.

Mattern, Joanne. *The History of Radio.* Berkley Heights, NJ: Enslow, 2003.

Smith, Anthony, and Richard Paterson. *Television: An International History.* New York: Oxford University Press, 1998.

Videos and DVDs

The Golden Age of TV Comedy—Favorite Television Classics. Los Angeles: Delta Entertainment Corporation, 2003.

Ken Burns' America: Empire of the Air. New York: PBS, 1991.

Rock 'N' Roll Invaders: The AM Radio DJs. New York: Winstar Home Entertainment, 1998.

Vietnam: A Television History. Boston: PBS, 1997.

Web Sites

history.acusd.edu/gen/recording/radio-television0.html A detailed site about the history of radio and TV.

members.aol.com/jeff560/jeff.html A comprehensive site covering the history of American broadcasting.

www.californiahistoricalradio.com This site is devoted to old radio programs.

www.mtr.org/ The official site of the Museum of Television and Radio in New York, which preserves classic radio and television programs.

www.rtvf.unt.edu/links/histsites.htm A site with links to many sites about the history of radio and TV.

INDEX

47

Author Biography

Michael Teitelbaum has been a writer and editor of children's books and magazines for over twenty-five years. In addition to his fiction work with characters ranging from *Garfield* to *Spider-Man*, Michael's most recent nonfiction books include *Great Moments in Women's Sports* (a title in the Wolrd Almanac Library *Great Moments in Sports* series), *Chinese Immigration,* and biographies of James Monroe and Herbert Hoover. Michael and his wife, Sheleigh, split their time between New York City and their 170-year-old farmhouse in the Catskill Mountains of upstate New York.